This book belongs to:

____

____

____

1

Alethia was a lively and healthy little girl who lived in a big city with her family.

The blocks of offices, flats and apartments in the city were so tall and from the windows you could look out and see for miles into the distance.

At night the lights from the tall buildings twinkled brightly. At sunrise a beautiful golden glow shone reflected from the glass windows all around!

3

When there were fireworks on various special
days in the year, Alethia and her family would
spend hours looking at the spectacular displays
from the top floor of their house.

They would gasp- 'oooh' and 'ahhhh' as the dark
sky brightened with all of the colours of the
rainbow .

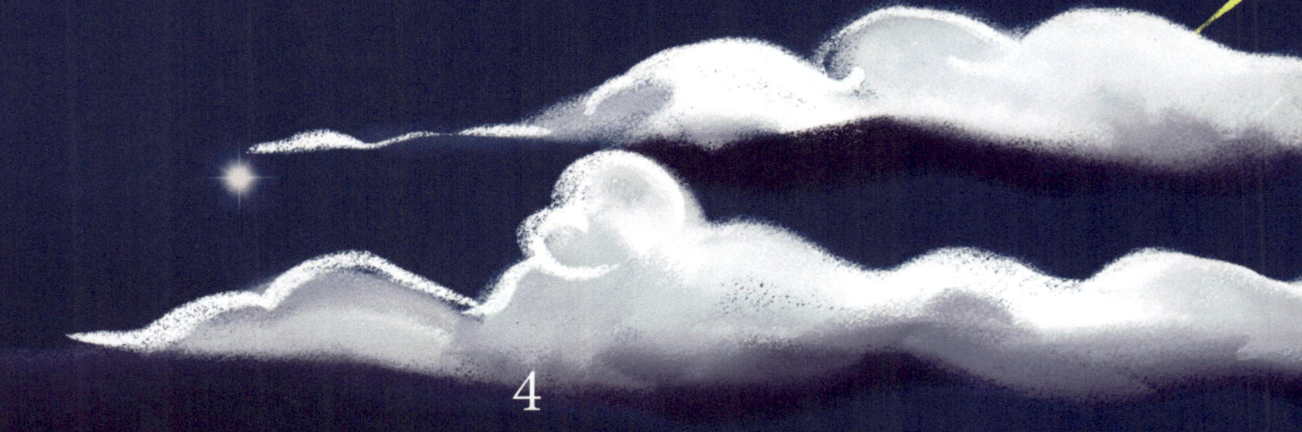

Alethia's grandparents were both from the
beautiful Caribbean island of Jamaica,
known for its high mountains,
beautiful beaches and musically
talented people.

They travelled from the tropical
paradise - where fruit and vegetables
grew in abundance, to work in
England in the 1950's.

England was cold with
grey skies when they
disembarked the ship
with so many other
enthusiastic young
people from the
Caribbean.

8

PEGRAMS

They rented a small room in the City
close to the hospital where they were
able to get jobs. Her Mum was a nurse
and her Dad was an engineer.

10

11

Alethia was the fourth child of five, she had three brothers and one sister. Alethia would enjoy playing with her siblings inside the hallways and out in the garden of their home.

It was so much fun! They dressed up, sang joyful songs and acted in short plays they had created with other children in the neighbourhood.

Alethia loved school and her hand
would often shoot in the air to answer
the teacher's questions.

Her eyes would sparkle as she waited to
hear her name called out and she usually
got the correct answers!

Alethia was very confident and was quite strong for her age. She could run very fast and would often win races against other children in her year.

Alethia strived for excellence in secondary school. She would read her books and always did her homework neatly and on time.

Her teachers were very happy with the homework she handed in. She would always get marks of 9 out of 10 or 10 out of 10!

When her teachers were happy, Alethia was happy!

19

Alethia thought for a long time about what she should do when she was grown up.

Her teachers told her she should go to university because she had so much potential!

21

Alethia realised that some children in her school were not always brushing their teeth as they should. Eating sugary food meant that sometimes their teeth had small holes or cavities which could painful!

She saw that in older people, teeth could become wobbly and break especially if they had not looked after their teeth when they were young.

Alethia wanted to help others to look after their teeth and keep them straight and clean.

She decided that she wanted to study to become a dentist and an orthodontist. She had always liked to brush her own teeth, keeping them clean and giving her a brilliant smile.

At first the teachers were not
very sure that she was able
to do all of the hard work
that was needed to become a
dentist.

However, Alethia made sure
that she applied to a dental
school and worked hard to get
the necessary Advanced-level
grades in her school subjects!

When Alethia was 17, she received the news that the had achieved the grades she needed! She had to decide whether she wanted go to work or leave her family to go to university.

There were plenty of jobs available and she could have gone to work in a bank or in an office. Certainly, the money she would earn from a job could be given to her Mummy and Daddy so they could use it to buy clothes and food for the large family.

On the other hand, she enjoyed learning and really wanted to study more. She wanted to become a dentist!

BANK
29

She was so happy to start the course which took four years to complete. There was lots of time spent in the classroom and looking into patients' mouths to make sure their teeth and gums were healthy.

At dental school, Alethia learned
how to deal with cavities, infections
and how to take out bad teeth.

She encouraged patients to eat
healthily, brush their teeth using the
correct techniques and good quality
toothpaste.

She wanted to make sure that the
enamel, dentine and the gums were
protected from decay and disease.

33

With good teeth, patients are able to smile nicely and chew their food to digest it properly!

Once Alethia completed dental school, she became a dentist for few years before going back to University and completing a Masters degree - to become an orthodontist. She did very well!

This meant that she would specialise in straightening crooked teeth, both in children and in adults so that they could have a nice smile.

Alethia always does excellent work for her patients. They are always very happy with the results of nice straight teeth and lovely smile!

They can smile and be confident with their family, school friends, work colleagues and customers.

37

Alethia has become a dedicated dentist and orthodontist. She enjoys helping people have healthy and straight teeth.

Maybe you could become a dentist or orthodontist one day, just like her!

If you want to be a dedicated dentist and, take a look at these references to learn how!

<u>For Kids:</u>

Kids Britannica
Kids Britannica page on dentistry.
https://kids.britannica.com/kids/article/dentist/611077

Kiddle
Kiddle encyclopedia page on dentistry.
https://kids.kiddle.co/Dentistry

BBC bitesize
BBC bitesize page on teeth.
https://www.bbc.co.uk/bitesize/topics/z7x78xs/articles/zsp76yc

Weebly
GCSE page on teeth and tooth decay.

https://biology-igcse.weebly.com/human-teeth-and-dental-decay.html

<u>For parents and guardians:</u>

UCAS
UCAS website for studying dentistry in the UK.
https://www.ucas.com/explore/subjects/dentistry

University Expert
University Expert page on helping your child get into dentistry.
https://universityexpert.co.uk/how-to-help-your-child-get-into-dentistry/

Wellsmile
Information page on the dental specialty of orthodontics.
https://www.wellsmile.co.uk/schools/career-in-orthodontics/

Colgate
Career pathway to becoming an orthodontist.
https://www.colgate.com/en-us/oral-health/adult-orthodontics/how-to-

become-an-orthodontist

What do you want to be when you grow up? Draw it
below!

Notes!

Check out some other books in the series!

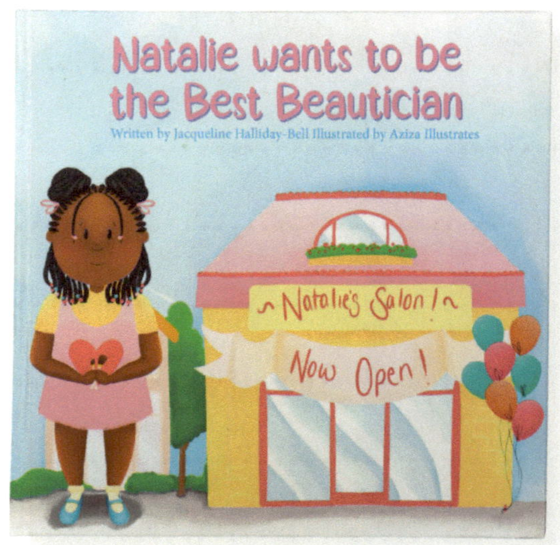